Re:LIFE & The Myth of Motivation

Ed Kang

Copyright 2009 Ed Kang

ISBN 978-0-557-11694-2

John,
Thank-you for all your love.

Re:LIFE & The Myth of Motivation

Ed   Nov 9, 2009

To my wife Tae-Young,
you remind me how amazing Life is,
thank you for your faith for me
even when I had little faith for myself.

To my sons Orlando and Julian,
someday you will read this on your own
and I pray you will truly understand
what Life has in store for you both.

WELCOME: MR. WOODCOCK & YOUR LIFE

Mr. Woodcock:

"So what's your book about?"

John Farley:

"It teaches people how they can release painful memories so they can rebuild their self-esteem."

Mr. Woodcock:

"Lot of losers out there I guess."

— From the movie, *Mr. Woodcock*

One night, I was tapping away on my laptop with the television on in the background. The movie, *Mr. Woodcock*, starring Billy Bob Thornton and Sean William Scott, came on the channel. If you have never heard of the movie before, don't worry. I don't think it was a blockbuster hit, but I remembered the previews being funny. So, being a big fan of both Billy Bob and Sean William Scott, I decided to indulge myself.

The movie was about a self-help guru, John Farley (Sean William Scott), who had just achieved national acclaim with the publishing of his book, *Letting Go: Getting Past Your Past*. As the hero of our story travels the country on a book tour, he decides to go back to his hometown to see his mother and accept a prestigious local award. It is there he finds that his childhood nemesis, Mr. Woodcock (Billy Bob Thornton), has been dating his mother. Mr. Woodcock was John's high school gym teacher from hell who preyed upon weakness and humiliated him in class for being one among what he termed a "disgrace to fat, gelatinous, out-of-shape little kids the world over." John Farley had to dig deep into his own self-help advice and overcome his own painful past in what turned out to be a pretty entertaining movie.

I was drawn to this movie for two reasons. First, it did a great job of poking fun at the self-help-publishing industry. There were scenes of lineups at bookstores of teary people telling the author, "Your book saved my life!" His book hit a personal chord, which could be considered self-help. Second, as over-the-top as he was, we all have a Mr. Woodcock in our lives in some form—many of us don't even know it.

Everywhere I go, I engage with people about their lives and have identified a few common personal issues. For the most part, people's challenges seem to fall into three categories:

Feeling lost or stuck;

Feeling regret;

Feeling like there should be something more.

I am not the only one who has observed these commonalities. There are a great deal of resources out there to address these three main areas from very qualified sources. But for me, even though I do work with people in these very challenges, the bigger problem is the fact that most feel like losers or being of less value for experiencing the feelings they do.

Feeling like a loser is the real danger here.

This is a danger that petrifies us and steals the purpose, passion, and potential in our lives. The only power our Mr. Woodcocks of the world have is the ability to convince people they are losers and have no hope to become otherwise.

The quote at the beginning of the chapter from the movie represents the crux of what I am referring to here. I hate to admit it, but I had to stifle a good chuckle when I saw the above-mentioned scene. (I laughed for real when he threw the best-selling book into the fireplace.)

We all have questions in our hearts. I firmly believe those questions deserve answers before anything else. Unfortunately, the Mr. Woodcocks of the world make us feel invalidated in these desires and deter us from embarking on a journey of self-explo-ration and personal freedom. This book will give you permission to do just that.

Another common experience in my interactions with people is facing the question on whether I am some type of coach. I recognize that the life-coaching industry has experienced a boom in recent years, but I cringe when clumped into this group. This is partly because I have some issues in general with the self-help and motivational industry, which will be explained shortly. But the title "coach" really makes me queasy because of people's potentially unhealthy expectations — the title somehow puts me on a pedestal.

You will see that I have no qualifications to really help anybody except for my will to be as transparent as possible about my own learning experiences. I have made choices in my life that are both positive and hurtful. But no matter how these decisions turned out, I have tried to learn from them and harness those lessons for the benefit of others — you included.

This journey has been nothing short of incredible. I am thankful for my family and the community around me that have embraced the vision and joined together in building and changing communities. We are seeing lives transformed all around the world, which is the true reward, because it amounts to more than any possible accolades that I could get for publishing a book.

Do you feel lost, stuck, or regretful?

Or do you feel there should be something more?

How so?

Have you ever had a Mr. Woodcock in your life?

Who was it, and what did he or she say?

How did that affect you?

> **"Life is a verb, not a noun."**
> —Charlotte Perkins Gilman

Contents

INTRODUCTION: AN AIRBORNE CONFESSIONAL	1
DESTINY: IS RE:LIFE FOR YOU?	13
OUR CORE NEEDS: RESULTS & RELATIONSHIPS	17
RECOGNIZE: THE INVISIBLE CONFLICT	21
RECOGNIZE: GAPS OF A FEATHER ...	31
REFRAME: REGARD FOR LIFE	37
REFRAME: WHAT RE:LIFE IS NOT	45
REFRAME: COMPARING THE GAP & LIFE	55
RESPOND: THE GAP STRIKES BACK	59
RESPOND: THE FOUR-STEP METHOD TO LIFE	67
REFLECT: THREE CIRCLES OF RE:LIFE	81
REFLECT: RE:LIFE RE:LATIONAL	97
REFLECT: RE:LIFE FINANCIAL	105
REFLECT: LIFE IN LOCKDOWN	111
REFLECT: THE RE:LIFE RESPONSIBILITY	117
NEXT STEPS: ADDITIONAL RESOURCES & ACKNOWLEDGMENTS	121

INTRODUCTION: AN AIRBORNE CONFESSIONAL

"Most truths are so naked that people feel sorry for them and cover them up, at least a little bit."

—Edward R. Murrow

In March of 2009, I found myself on a plane heading to Nicaragua. The purpose of my trip was to embark on a so-called journey of compassion with the human-itarian organization Impact Nations. On the plane departing from my home in Calgary, I was sitting beside Jodie, a longtime friend and colleague. Across the aisle were Melissa and Rose, who were also friends of my family and part of the team.

The tragic irony was that although I was on a mission to change the world with this group of wonderful people, not one of them really knew just how messed up my own life was.

So I decided there was really nothing better to do than spend the next few hours getting it all off my chest starting with whomever would listen: Jodie was the unenviable first. I'm pretty sure she knew something was amiss. But like the good friend I always remembered her to be, she let me bend her ear in a million different directions as I disclosed to her my personal junk like a devout and guilt-ridden Catholic sitting in an airborne confessional.

Our journey of compassion consisted of opening seven medical clinics with feeding centers in the poorest regions of Nicaragua. Our home base was the city Chinandega, which reportedly had the highest rate of crime, prostitution, alcohol abuse, and suicide. The team consisted of roughly twenty-two men and women from an array of diverse backgrounds; it included teenagers, professionals of all kinds, and retired nurses. As a whole, we were coming together as representatives from four different countries, which in my mind was very encouraging.

This trip was extremely important to me because I was on what you could call a detox from my life. I had just spent two years working as the chief operations officer for a new publicly traded business development and holdings corporation. As we fought for the company's survival and success, I pursued a personal passion of mine by working as a teacher and a high school chaplain. Previously I was an associate pastor at a church on the local university campus.

By that time, however, I was pretty much burnt out and done with my life.

When I say "done," I really mean it. Between the career stress and pressures of being a good husband and father, I had become an adrenaline-addicted fly-by-the-seat-of-my-pants workaholic. I was burning my life and every relational bridge I could identify. My wife was mad at me. My partners were mad at me. And it didn't take very long for my clients and business acquaintances to also become mad at me.

I was not a happy person.

In fact, before I left for Nicaragua, I wrote a confessional letter to my business partner and longtime friend, Donnie, giving him a completely clear look into the disastrous state of affairs that was called my life. I also just signed some checks and gave my bank cards to Jordan, another partner and friend, clearly instructing him that I wanted absolutely no communication during my time in Central America. I had my phone with me, but I vowed not to check my e-mails or messages for the two weeks I was away. This was excruciating for the first three days, but after the initial shakes and jitters, I was happy I made that commitment. It didn't help that yet another business partner, Chad, had to pick up all the slack and get buried under my unmet responsibilities. There were more loose ends in my life than the back of a wall-sized tapestry. I can't thank Tae-Young—my wife—Donnie, Jordan, and Chad enough for bearing the brunt of my personal implosion and silently suffering while I was gone.

All I knew was that secretly, I wished I never had to come back to Calgary and confront all the issues that would pounce on me like paparazzi on a celebrity scandal upon my return.

How did I get into that situation? I'd like to say that it wasn't by choice, but I have to take full unadulterated responsibility and say it was.

Everything in my life had become all about me, and that's what got me in really deep trouble.

Now the majority who knew me had no idea what was going on. In fact, some assumed I was living the dream in many ways. There was a lot of prestige and recognition in what I did. But if you were on the inside, it was not a pretty picture.

Imagine a train chugging along at high speed and pulling a few dozen cars filled to the brim. Imagine the faster that train goes, the more cars it tries to pick up. Why? Because that's what good trains do, right?

Now imagine that the head engine car of the train decides to abruptly stop. What do you think happens to the rest of that train? It gets really ugly. My life was that train, and I just knew, sitting on my Nicaragua-bound plane, I was on a personal crash course of total disaster.

But the reality was I needed to be completely derailed before I could experience the miracles of what transpired in the next fourteen days.

My Nicaraguan journey of compassion changed my life completely.

Out of the flaming debris and complete carnage that was my life, something amazing was to emerge. Somehow I was given a clean slate and a second chance. A new perspective was gifted to me while I stood in garbage dumps and even prisons serving those ravaged by poverty and injustice. I came face-to-face with both the light and dark sides of humanity within and around me. And when that occurs, you have no choice but to change.

Boy, did I ever change!

Not to say that I instantly turned into a saint or started walking and talking like Mother Teresa. I genuinely wish it was that easy. No way. The truth about a detox is that it only gives you a momentary window of clarity and lucidity to make some really tough decisions. I had a lot more work to do, and I still am working on it to this day.

There is a big difference between me and one who has a chemical or substance addiction. At least if you are an alcohol or drug addict, you can try detox, for the most part, and avoid contact with the source of addiction. The problem for me was I was addicted to something far more nefarious and damaging.

I was addicted to *people's opinions*.

At this point, you may have the inclination to scoff and bury this little book into a deep dark hole, or throw it into the fireplace like Mr. Woodcock did. Addiction to people's opinions? Am I kidding? No. I can't explain my addiction any other way. There is also one other truth that may completely throw you over the edge: we all have the same addiction.

Think about this for a second. I believe we are all born with addictive personalities in some form or another. But no other addiction is more popular and powerful than that of the opinions of others.

We spend our entire lives going through addictive behaviors like trying to make other people happy and gaining approval by meeting standards of good externally prescribed for us.

From the moment we are born, we are thrust into a childhood where we crave hearing the words, "Good boy!" or "Good girl!" When we are in school, we strive for good grades. Upon leaving the halls of umpteen years of education, we undergo severe anxiety trying to attain good careers and good relationships. We then put on brave faces and earnestly attempt to be good parents with matching good families. This starts the cycle all over again by passing down the addictions to our children for many years to come.

We are afraid to be rejected by those who hold the standards of what is good over us like judgments delivered from some unholy high court. Whether it is our parents, co-workers, managers, successful people we look up to, figures we idolize, or even church leaders in holy sanctuaries, we are always trying to make somebody happy or meet some cultural ideal.

What happens when we fail at pleasing people or meeting these standards? There is disappointment, of course. And like any good addict, we self-medicate. This is done either through pushing even harder and using our recent performance as the latest addiction hit, or we withdraw to avoid future pain and find comfort in other vices—this is where real substance abuse and other conditions like gambling, eating disorders, and pornography find their foothold.

This book is about overcoming this addiction to what is thought of as *good*.

This is not to say there are no good and bad things in life that should be sought or avoided. Sunshine, puppies, hugs, and that sound your golf club makes when you hit the ball just right are definitely good things. Gunshot wounds, toxic waste, parking tickets, and having the hot water abruptly run out while you are doing your best *American Idol* impersonation in the shower are definitely bad ones.

Nor am I saying that the pursuit of a good career, a good family, and, in general, a good life is something bad. My argument is that if the standard of good is derived from other people's expectations or from popular culture and it does not resonate in tune with our hearts and souls, something is terribly wrong. And if we pursue this good like junkies, burning ourselves and others for that next high, then it becomes an addiction that produces many of the so-called walking dead we see around us. By the term "walking dead" I mean those that seem to just exist with no purpose and passion in life.

Maybe this doesn't apply to you, and that's fine. This book isn't for people who think they are strong and healthy. Nothing I say would penetrate their world anyway. This is for those who find their own trains are about to crash any minute and are starting to get really honest with themselves. Or it's for those who have already burnt out and are now just slowly dying from the inside out.

I found hope, and so can you.

What happened in Nicaragua? If you can just hang on and wait until the end of this book, you will understand how my life was completely redeemed and other's lives transformed.

In no way is my world today a bed of roses. I still struggle just like any normal guy out there. A recovering alcoholic reminds himself he is an addict for the rest of his life. This doesn't mean that person has not achieved victory over the addiction. It's a gesture of humility to accept that at any time one can fall right back into the addictive patterns that destroyed his or her happiness in the first place.

I am an addict for life. And that's fine by me because former addicts can help other addicts. They have a message of sincere authenticity and can be a guide on the road less travelled.

All that being said, I have never been more excited about life in a very long time. I now serve as the executive chaplain and director for a business conglomerate called the Goliath Group of Companies. I have been reinvigorated with purpose and passion alongside my personal friend and mentor, Steve Casey, the head honcho at the Goliath Group. Steve had the compassion and wisdom to put me in a spiritual padded room while I squirmed and screamed from the shakes and shivers. Steve did this by having the insight to financially make my Nicaraguan adventure of transformation possible.

Through the Goliath Group, Steve and I are in the business of transformation — the transformation of business and the world. I personally live to see people conquer the Goliaths in their lives and experience true transformation.

I have also salvaged my old business partnerships into real friendships, and they've become more fulfilling than ever before. I now consider friends like Donnie as brothers-in-arms that share a foundation of friendship that you just don't find in regular companies. Although we may be in separate ventures or even parts of the world, we share a common vision to see real change — the kind of change that leaves a legacy we can all be proud of.

This book is called *Re:LIFE* because it is about a newfound regard for life that has become the focus for a growing community of people. We all have discovered each other, simply through living by conviction and exploring an alternative to the safe, cushy, and good life. Every day I wake up thanking God for the privilege and honor to have crossed their paths. Sometimes I go to bed at night completely in awe, speechless, and wondering to myself, *What did I do to deserve this?* For the first time in years, I don't feel lost in my calling but as someone who yearns to leave the world a better place than when he entered it.

Re:LIFE was a gift given to me by some very special people over the course of many years and hardships. And now I wish to share it with you.

May it breathe a new hope, vision, and freedom to pursue everything you imagined and were destined for—just like it is doing for me and for many others.

DESTINY:
IS RE:LIFE FOR YOU?

"Life is the childhood for our immortality."

—Johann Wolfgang Von Goethe

We all have a destiny—you included.

Destiny means something different for everybody. For some, destiny is something we cannot change, no matter what we do or how hard we try. Destiny, framed in this context, is like a narrow one-way road with no choice or escape. In my opinion, this is a pretty disheartening and cruel way to live.

Then there are others who don't consider destiny relevant at all. The concept of destiny is just too removed and distant from the grind of daily living. Being solely focused on the here and the now, the concept of a future vision of what we might become is just too far of a reach. In my opinion, this way of seeing the world is just far too shallow and unfulfilling.

So what is the true meaning of destiny? Here's what dictionary.com says about the word "destiny":

Destiny –noun

1. something that is to happen or has happened to a particular person or thing; lot or fortune.

2. the predetermined, usually inevitable or irresistible, course of events.

3. the power or agency that determines the course of events.

I have a different take on the above definition. I like to approach the concept of destiny like a blueprint designed by a master architect. We each have a unique blueprint that serves as the starting point to build something that pays tribute to the original designer. But the difference is it is up to *us* to decide whether or not we will build based on the blueprint.

In the Academy Award-winning movie *Slumdog Millionaire*, a "Who Wants to be a Millionaire" type question is posed that considers a similar view of destiny:

Jamal Malik is one question away from winning 20 million rupees. How did he do it?

A. He cheated.

B. He's lucky.

C. He's a genius.

D. It is written.

Was our main protagonist destined to win twenty million rupees? I won't ruin it for those who haven't seen it. But throughout the movie, Jamal made positive choices that granted him certain knowledge, which in turn allowed him to advance in the game show.

Jamal was building on the blueprint of his destiny.

Are you making the choice to do the same?

What if Jamal hadn't made the choices he did? The obvious is he wouldn't have been able to answer any of the questions. For example, when he gives a blind friend a $100 bill he received from a wealthy couple, the blind boy tells him the name of the president on the bill. This allows Jamal to answer the question on the televised game show. The host thought there was no way Jamal had ever even seen an American $100 bill let alone know the name Benjamin Franklin. What if Jamal had not been so generous and benevolent?

While *Slumdog Millionaire* may just be an entertaining work of fiction, I believe it was so widely popular because the principles of destiny behind the story are true. We do have a destiny we can build on—it is written.

Do you want to discover and build upon your destiny?

If you do, *Re:Life* is for you.

OUR CORE NEEDS: RESULTS & RELATIONSHIPS

"I don't want to get to the end of my life and find that I have lived just the length of it. I want to have lived the width of it as well."

— Diane Ackerman

Re:LIFE is for *everybody*.

I don't say this to try and break the *New York Times* best-seller list. I make this claim because at the end of the day, we are all people with two distinct core needs: results and relationships.

Results are based upon our desire for significance — to know we can and will make a difference. We want to see the significance in our lives increase by achieving real results. This is completely different from sitting around and believing we are somehow significant. That's just not good enough. We all need to know that there are tangible results to achieve and celebrate. Whether it be through accomplishments, challenges that we overcome, or recognition and status, results are undeniably important.

At the same time, everybody wants to feel like they are not alone—that they are in secure and meaningful relationships. While some deal with loneliness better than others, for the most part, we desire to be connected with people and communities around us in the context of authenticity and trust. Whether it is through family, a circle of friends, church groups, or that special someone, we all desire to love and be loved on a deeper level than just people passing each other on the street.

So what are you looking for?

Looking to see some results?

Results come in various forms and are valued differently by different people. Are you looking to be promoted at the office and increase your compensation? Maybe you want to achieve results to accelerate your career and professional life? Or are you an entrepreneur who enjoys the lifestyle freedoms from achieving greater results in your business? Or are you trying to reach personal goals in health, relationships, and finances? Maybe you are someone who has tried all the self-help and motivational resources out there to no avail.

Re:LIFE will help you achieve real results.

Are you feeling unsatisfied in your relationships?

Maybe you are currently in a relationship that needs improvement. Or maybe you feel lost in relationships altogether and don't know where to start. Let's face it; relationships are getting more complicated by the minute in our hypernetworked and trend-saturated culture. When it comes to romance, the standard boy-meets-girl fairy tale is virtually extinct. And when it comes to families, the steady increase in divorce rates and behavioural disorders that crop up at younger and younger ages are evidence enough of this increasing complexity.

Re:LIFE is all about helping you build real and secure relationships. So whether it is results or relationships, *Re:LIFE* will address your core needs of security and significance. But let me give you a bit of a warning:

Results and relationships go together; you cannot have one without the other.

On one hand, there are many people who sacrifice healthy relationships to maximize results. This is a blunder that ends up costing us in the long-run. There will always come a time when our capacity for results will diminish. In other words, the older we get, the less we are able to perform in the same ways we did in the past. We are then left with only one thing: you guessed it ... relationships!

You just don't see executives and CEOs on their deathbeds sweating over the few percentage points they lost or how many more hours they should have spent at the office. At the end of life, we want relationships more than anything to be by our side because relationships mean memories, and memories mean we will always leave something cherished behind.

On the other hand, there are others who become so consumed by relationships, their capacity to be effective is stunted. These are individuals who spend more time caring about whether or not they are accepted in the workplace than getting any work done. These are individuals who are so preoccupied with romance or a significant other that they miss out on a whole world of personal development and opportunities. An unhealthy imbalance toward relationships can lead to codependence. And it is out of codependence that we spawn abuse and neglect—the two sinister root causes of a failed relationship.

Re:LIFE is about finding harmony and complete fulfillment between results and relationships.

RECOGNIZE: THE INVISIBLE CONFLICT

"A mind all logic is like a knife all blade. It makes the hand bleed that uses it."

—Rabindranath Tagore

There is an invisible conflict we all must face every minute of the day. This conflict is invisible because it happens internally in the realm between thought and emotion. You could say this conflict is spiritual in nature because we cannot tangibly see it or touch it. But believe me, the fruits of this conflict, both positive and negative, are very real.

This conflict is between two seeds of motivation we all inherit from our collective human condition when one is born.

The first seed of motivation is based on the image of our true design and blueprint. It is the repre-ssentation of our authentic selves that motivates us to pursue lives of purpose and passion. This seed is what motivates us to live and love. I call this the seed of Life-based motivation. We will visit what this Life really is in a moment.

The second seed of motivation is based on a myth. I call it the Myth of Motivation. The Myth of Motivation is essentially a deception that causes us to focus inward and judge ourselves in the context of what is considered bad or good. The following is a definition of the word "myth" as found in dictionary.com.

Myth – noun

1. a traditional or legendary story, usually concerning some being or hero or event, with or without a determinable basis of fact or a natural explanation, esp. one that is concerned with deities or demigods and explains some practice, rite, or phenomenon of nature.

2. stories or matter of this kind: *realm of myth.*

3. any invented story, idea, or concept: *His account of the event is pure myth.*

4. an imaginary or fictitious thing or person.

The roots of myth are found in knowledge. I am not referring to text-book knowledge like mathematics or how to program your iPod. By "knowledge," I mean the evidence that leads us into judgment of whether something or someone is good or bad.

The distance between what we perceive to be good or bad is what I call the Gap.

The real trap behind the Myth of Motivation is that somehow we can *fix* or *fill* the Gap. This is impossible for the simple reason that we are not perfect and consequently there will always be a Gap between where we are and where we feel we should be. The same goes for how we perceive the world around us. There will always be a Gap between where everyone and everything else stands and our expectations of where they should be.

The most devastating aspect is that the Gap is filled with nothing but a tainted mixture of *shame* and all its related by-products. In this mixture are forms of selfishness, guilt, fear, anger, stress, anxiety, and even paranoia. These are the natural reactions to falling short of the concept of good in the Gap. These are the results of being constantly inwardly focused because of our knowledge of good and bad. Because we have knowledge of good, we have no choice but to judge ourselves, and feel judged, by how far we are from bad. This inward focus deceives us from all that life really has to offer. The following is a definition of the word "shame" from dictionary.com.

Shame – noun

1. the painful feeling arising from the consciousness of something dishonorable, improper, ridiculous, etc., done by oneself or another: *She was overcome with shame.*
2. susceptibility to this feeling: *to be without shame.*
3. disgrace; ignominy: *His actions brought shame upon his parents.*
4. a fact or circumstance bringing disgrace or regret: *The bankruptcy of the business was a shame. It was a shame you couldn't come with us.*

We instinctively know the Gap is killing us, and we work diligently trying to fix ourselves (or others) and fill the Gap by achieving what the world tells us is an accepted standard of good. This culminates in that addiction to people's opinions I described in the introduction. It also results in the futile pursuit of cultural perfection that falsely pressures us through popular media and collective social expectations.

Speaking of media, advertising is built completely upon leveraging the Gap. Frontal assaults based on the Gap come from everywhere, but I like to pick on the beauty and fashion industries. When we are bombarded with images of men and women who have achieved a physical state really only possible through genetic proclivity, what are we led to believe? How about those commercials with buxom women talking about the little pill that enhances that certain part of the male body? Where do our minds go? We think about how far we have fallen short of a good state of physical perfection or sexual prowess, of course! This motivates us to purchase diet supplements and blue pills, order videos, and overall feel completely guilty about our bodies.

Even more subtle are the media messages that focus on the relational Gap. I am both intrigued and appalled by matchmaking Web site commercials. Again, when our senses are peppered with images and ideas of romance and living happily ever after, what's really going on? The Gap! Quite frankly, this type of advertising only contributes to the desperate approach to romance that has made dating and courtship extremely difficult for many.

To again simplify it all, there are only two sources of motivation in our lives: Gap and Life. There is nothing in between.

The Gap always asks the following question:

How far is this from good, and how can I fix it?

Anytime you feel yourself judging by how far something or someone has fallen from some expectation of good, you are being motivated by the Gap. The same goes for anytime you feel judged or are judging yourself based on how far you have fallen from good. Typically this is accompanied by one of the shame-based emotions described just a moment ago.

The Gap is everywhere. It is revealed almost every minute of our lives because it is a part of who we are. Nobody escapes the two seeds of motivation. The Gap is ingrained into every fibre of our existence. And thus, our entire culture has become about trying to fix and fill the Gap.

I hate to say it, but even the institution of church is guilty of propagating the Gap. I should know. At one point I was a pastor who thought my job description was to fix people and help them become good according to our interpretations of the Bible. I am not saying that church is bad. In fact, I believe the true intention and essence of the church is to be a loving faith-based community which can be one of the most beautiful things in this world. What I am saying is that *motivation matters* and that the majority of those that participate in institutional religion are motivated to do so because of a perceived Gap of how far they have fallen short of a personal and spiritual standard of good.

I speak with many individuals who attend church out of the guilt and fear that they will not be considered as spiritual as the others who attend every week. I wonder how God feels about this. From my standpoint, I would rather have a group of people congregate because of love rather than some sense of obligation. And I'm pretty sure from my own experience and personal exploration, God shares the same view.

Let's look at other examples of being motivated by the Gap. These are all hypothetical situations based upon my past experiences working with people. Any similarities in this entire book to you or anybody you know are completely coincidental—unless of course the example is about me.

A young professional can't seem to take any feedback from management and tends to get hostile or depressed when his performance is under review. This young man is acting out of a Gap that says his value in life is solely determined by how good he is at his job.

A couple, despite lacking the financial resources, decides to put their children in a private school because the rest of their community does the same. But they find they are relentlessly bickering at the dinner table and making the kids feel guilty. This family has made Gap-based decisions at the cost of their own happiness.

A young student suddenly finds she is very upset and frustrated because of a realization that all her life she has been trying to follow in her family's footsteps by being a medical professional and that all the time she has only loathed her program of study. This Gap of trying to fulfill family expectations is very common.

A husband of ten years wants a divorce because he has lost his job and now his wife supports the family as the primary breadwinner. The fact that his spouse now seems more successful than he is has created a massive Gap of where he believes he was supposed to be as a family provider and husband.

A young man is considered a leader in his personal and professional circles but is living a dual life of secret addictions. Inside he is screaming for help, but the Gap between where he is and where he believes his community expects him to be is continuing his spiral further and further into darkness.

A manager of a corporate firm just cannot muster up the courage to fire certain employees who are affecting the overall productivity. His Gap-based fear is that he will be seen as a terrible manager. Instead he hurts the entire company by avoiding confrontation and remaining passive when strong leadership is required.

A mother harshly scolds her children for embarrassing behaviour in public. Her motivation is based upon the fear that those around them may perceive her as an unfit mother because the children are misbehaved. Out of her feeling of shame, she in turn shames others, which in the long run produce the exact opposite of obedience and respect.

I am sure you can begin to identify you own examples. I would like you to begin recognizing the possible personal Gaps and the Gaps in the world around you. Do you see them? The more proficient you become at recognizing Gaps, the better you will be at taking the proactive steps to eliminate their power.

Then you will be able to move to the next step: Life.

Have you recognized a Gap or Myth of Motivation in your life so far? Describe what it might be or where it might have come from.

RECOGNIZE: GAPS OF A FEATHER ...

"Life is a long lesson in humility."

—James M. Barrie

The old saying goes, "Birds of a feather flock together." It's the same with Gap-based motivation. Gaps actually attract and feed off each other.

Typically when one person comes from a Gap-based motivation, those around him become Gap-based too. Say you have been offended by the poor service at a restaurant. Clearly you can pronounce judgement because they have fallen short of your expected standard of good, right? But what if you were to react on that perceived Gap and take it upon yourself to remind them how bad of a job they were doing? What do you think would be the response? Typically the server at fault would be reminded of her own Gap of how thankless the job can be. The service would most likely remain the same, or even worse, and some form of retaliation, such as unwanted ingredients, would appear in your food!

This is how something small can escalate into full-fledged Gap-based battles. When one person acts out of the Gap, the natural response in others is to react the same way. If somebody hurls an insult or criticism pointing out the Gap in our lives, our first inclination is to remind them of their own. Gaps feed off each other and create no-win situations for all parties.

The dangerous part is we can always find a way to silently justify Gap-based motivations and actions. Let me give you an example and true story that has happened a little too often.

I am trying to get some sleep before having to get up early for a stressful day at work. One of my sons begins to cry. What goes through my mind? Do I think about getting up and letting my wife sleep? For a moment, yes, but soon the Gap takes over. I begin thinking to myself that *I* am the one that *deserves* sleep, and if my wife would just be a good mother, I would be able to do my job the next day and be a good provider for the family. And when she doesn't respond to my expectations, I become disappointed and even offended that she does not see things the same way.

At that point, what do you think my wife is thinking? Well, of course, my Gap-based behavior has triggered another Gap-based response. She begins to think about how she has to take care of the kids all day while trying to keep the house clean and prepare dinner for a husband that gets to be outside, have adult conversations, and expects to come home to an orderly home. The Gap of how she is overworked and taken for granted grows and grows to the point where both of us sit quietly self-justified in an old-fashioned standoff, while our child's wailing becomes louder and louder.

Are both of us justified in our positions?

Absolutely.

But is there any victory or productive outcome to be had in that justification?

Absolutely not.

This is the danger of self-justified Gap-based behaviour. It puts others into their own Gap-based thinking.

Another way that Gaps attract each other is when someone takes the time to reveal how short another person has fallen from their picture of good out of the wrong motivation.

Let's use my marriage again as another example.

I am a big Ultimate Fighting Championship (UFC) fan. Few things get me more excited than the anticipation of a pay-per-view event where I can sit and cheer like a Roman at a gladiator coliseum. My problem is because I am a male that thinks in boxes and cannot multitask, during the event I tend to forget that I am married and have the associated family responsibilities.

A few times my wife would be struggling to take out the garbage or bring in some groceries during a UFC event. That particular night, she decides to comment something to the effect of, "Oh it must be nice to be able to do whatever you want in this family." And as I usually do, I fall for the trap and have a Gap-based reaction.

I should know what my wife is really trying to say is, "Honey, I would sure appreciate some consideration here." What I am interpreting is, "You are a bad husband and father, and I loathe the fact you like UFC." She is pointing out a Gap in me and asking me to fix it. Out of my own shame and insecurity, I take it personally.

So how do I react? I manage to go on a fifteen-minute tirade about how much stress I am experiencing at work, the lack of respect I feel in my marriage, and how the UFC keeps me sane and allows me to blow off steam. Of course I also remind her about where she has fallen short in areas that are typically inconsequential but become amplified when viewed through my Gap-based lens. The result is a round-robin of Gap-motivated blows and counterblows that frighten the children and reduce family conversations to one-word exchanges for the next forty-eight hours.

It doesn't stop there. After the initial incident, I am found furiously cleaning the entire house, muttering under my breath, "I'll show her I can be a good husband!" Do you think it helped? My wife is way smarter than that. She can see Gap-based motivations a mile away, and my attempts to make her feel guilty never do anything to diffuse the situation. The only thing that has ever worked in such situations is a sincere and loving apology from both of us.

So other than the fact I am nowhere near being a perfect husband, do you see how Gaps quickly pile up and make things worse? What's the solution? We're getting to that next!

Can you describe a situation where one Gap has attracted and fed another? How and why do you think it has happened?

REFRAME: REGARD FOR LIFE

"Life is a lot like a marathon. If you can finish a marathon, you can do anything you want."

—Oprah Winfrey

The solution to Gap is Life.

Life is the other seed of motivation that exists in our lives. The difference between Gap and Life is like the difference between night and day.

The Life-based motivation constantly asks one question:

How can I have a higher regard for Life?

This is where we combine the two words "regard" and "life" for the term "Re:LIFE." But a straightforward and obvious question you may have is, "What is Life?" Life is something we don't think about very much. Yet it permeates our worlds in every way. The following is a definition of the term "life" from dictionary.com.

Life – noun

1. the animate existence or period of animate existence of an individual: to risk one's life; a short life and a merry one.

2. a corresponding state, existence, or principle of existence conceived of as belonging to the soul: eternal life.

3. the general or universal condition of human existence: Too bad, but life is like that.

These are three of the twenty-five different noun definitions for the word "life." As you can see, it can have a great deal of different meanings, depending upon context and individual mindset. And that's what makes Life so special — it means something different for everyone. But if, for the sake of this discussion, I have to work out a concrete definition of the word Life, I would do it like this:

Life: The highest aspiration and expression of our love.

Sound cheesy? I can understand why one may feel like I pulled this out of a corny fortune cookie, but let's think about this. What is the single force in this world that truly advances Life? It's love. So to aspire to Life is to aspire to love. Love is the greatest motivation behind true Life. And the greatest expression Life has to offer is love. When we love something, we are deeming it worthy of all our lives.

So then what does it mean to have a *regard for life?* The following is what dictionary.com says about the word "regard."

Regard – verb

1. to look upon or think of with a particular feeling: *to regard a person with favor.*
2. to have or show respect or concern for.
3. to think highly of; esteem.
4. to take into account; consider.

When we look upon something or someone with respect or concern, we are not thinking of the Gap. When we think highly of something and place it on the same level of respect and concern as we want for ourselves, the power of the Gap is nullified. When we stop to take things into account and consider everything from a Life-based perspective, our insecurity, fear, doubt, and shame cease to have their power.

In other words, after one turns from the Gap, there is nothing left to do but to aspire to and express love for the sake of Life. Imagine a world without any Gaps. What would it be like to not live under judgment and condemnation of how far we fall short from good? How would people feel if they never felt like they had to fix themselves? Our greatest calling in Life is to love, and to love is to have the highest regard for Life.

Do you have a high regard for Life? I am certain you do, whether you describe it in my terms or not, or you wouldn't have read this far. What you have proven is that you at minimum have a very high regard for your own life. It's time to show you how that same regard can manifest itself in powerful ways to create abundance and freedom in you and the world around you. This is the gift!

There are two fruits of the seed of Life-based motivation: creation and redemption. These are the key success indicators of Re:LIFE. The following are the definitions found in dictionary.com of the words "create" and "redeem" respectively.

Create – verb

1. to cause to come into being, as something unique that would not naturally evolve or that is not made by ordinary processes.

2. to evolve from one's own thought or imagination, as a work of art or an invention.

3. To cause to happen; bring about; arrange, as by intention or design: *to create a revolution; to create an opportunity to ask for a raise.*

Redeem – verb

1. to buy or pay off; clear by payment: *to redeem a mortgage.*

2. to make up for; make amends for; offset (some fault, shortcoming, etc.): *His bravery redeemed his youthful idleness.*

3. to obtain the release or restoration of, as from captivity, by paying a ransom.

4. *Theology.* to deliver from sin and its consequences by means of a sacrifice offered for the sinner.

The difference between the act of creation and redemption is important. Re:LIFE is first about creating something new in Life, especially where there is no Life to begin with. When someone feels nothing but judgment and has lost all hope by falling into the Gap, there is an opportunity to create newness in Life. And this instinct to create is within us all.

For example, why do we, as humans, desire to have children? I can personally attest that there is no rational benefit at all for spawning offspring. They are messy, intrusive, and extremely self-centered. They make no substantial contribution to our lives. Yet, despite all this, I love my children more than myself.

Deep down, we love to create in Life. This is why we smile when a flower blooms or watch cute baby puppies in the window of a pet store.

Life is all about love, and love is all about Life.

On the other side of creation, there is redemption. For me, redemption is all about taking something that is dead, or deserves death, and transforming it for the sake of Life. Redemption is what happens when someone admits they have made a mistake and apologizes. Redemption is what happens when a victim forgives and releases the guilty party from responsibility.

Life is all about creation and redemption. The two together can overcome any Gap.

This is what Re:LIFE is all about. It's not about trying to fix or fill the Gap. It's actually about finding victory and freedom in our lives *despite* the Gap. When applied properly, the Gap really isn't a Gap at all. In fact, the Gap becomes an opportunity to *create* and *redeem* with the highest regard for Life.

I'd like to share with you an e-mail I received from my friend Megan. Megan is a

Re:LIFE leader and founding member of our Re:LIFE villages, which you will learn about a little later. Her story is the quintessential expression of what Life can do to create hope and redeem any circumstance. It is stories like this that provide a real Life-based motivation for me every day. This is how the e-mail goes:

> It started as a breakfast to catch up with an old University friend that I hadn't seen in over eight years. He asked a very simple question: "What would your average perfect day look like?" I remember thinking how basic this was but struggling to find the words to articulate a response.
>
> I don't know what I was seeking that day when I reconnected with Ed. Recently divorced, I was having to learn how to live on my own and manage the growing pains of finding who I was, separate from my husband, my family, and my friends. All I knew was that something told me that Ed would be an important piece to a puzzle: my life.
>
> Now, eighteen months later, I'm asked to share how Re:LIFE has affected me. How do I describe this? It is woven into the very fabric of my being—yes, I know this sounds corny, but bear with me. I have lived the last thirty-three years of my life desperately seeking acceptance and love from those who

I valued most in this world only to find that I was constantly falling short of their expectations. I lived my life based on Gap-based performance, filling the Gap by doing more, changing what was wrong with me, and still never feeling whole.

The question became, how do I shift from Gap to Life? The answer was simple. Surrender. Let go. Just choose Life. But it was easier said than done. Surrendering, letting go, Life are words more powerful than we give them credit for. Every moment, every decision, every relationship is viewed in the context of Life—the highest aspiration and expression of love.

Choosing Life and, in the process, enabling others to choose Life, has opened the door to my calling, my destiny, and my purpose. What can be more fulfilling than that? Now I remember that very first question that my friend asked me. What would my average perfect day look like? My response is, "Live every day out of love." That is the gift of Re:LIFE!

Do you have personal areas where you would like to see creation or redemption for the sake of Life? Can you describe them?

REFRAME: WHAT RE:LIFE IS NOT

> "We should take care not to make the intellect our god; it has, of course, powerful muscles, but no personality."
>
> — Albert Einstein

I've spent a bit of time extolling the virtues of Re:LIFE and demonstrating its potential application. I plan to provide a lot more practical insights of how to get Re:LIFE working for you. But before I continue, this is a good time to discuss what Re:LIFE is *not*.

The first reason to have this discussion is Re:LIFE is not bulletproof. It is not some magical mathe-matical equation that always spits out the same result no matter what you feed into it. Re:LIFE has its vulnerabilities. Having a high regard for Life is an attitude that can become twisted and even perverted if applied in the wrong context.

Re:LIFE will not make you a good person.

This may be obvious by now, but it is worth repeating. This is not about how bad you are or how you can move to being good.

Have you ever had someone shove a self-help book or magazine article on your face and say, "Read this; it will be good for you and you need it"? What's your first reaction? If you're like me, the first reaction is not so welcoming, because nobody likes being told they need to fill the Gap in their lives.

Let's think about why diets don't work. Statistically, diets, at best, cause nothing more than yo-yo weight loss and sometimes worse results in the long run. The commonly advertised concept of a diet implies you need to lose weight. That, ultimately, is interpreted as "You are fat," or "You don't look good in a swimsuit." And in our culture, if you don't fit the range of ideal body size, your perceived social value greatly diminishes.

The reaction is hundreds of well-intentioned yet unhealthy people making diet resolutions and hitting the gym with their new memberships and Lululemon outfits after New Year's. But how full are those gyms less than eight weeks later? That's right. They go back to normal business volumes. Gyms make profit on oversold memberships, not on people who actually use the gym.

Do you know what the difference is between those that just temporarily get in shape and those that always stay fit? Those who succeed have made their health choices about Life. Many—without even knowing the Myth of Motivation—make fitness about how much more regard for Life they can have by being healthy. My father is a great example. He used to smoke and eat whatever he wanted until he found a new Life motivation to become healthy. He channelled his efforts of getting fit with a community that enjoyed Life-based activities in relationships and nature activities. My father enjoyed these relationships so much that he could overcome any of his old habits simply by being in love with his outdoor gang.

I remember walking through a bookstore one day and seeing a big display with a new book entitled, *Become a Better You*. Do you know what my initial knee-jerk reaction was? I wanted to pick up the book and figure out what was wrong with me and learn how to fix it. Then I quickly realized I had just fallen into my own Gap. I started to get angry. I was angry because, although I have nothing personal against the author, I knew thousands of people would fall into their own Gaps and try to become better people only to be thwarted by the Myth of Motivation.

The same principle here applies to this book. If you are reading this because you think you are somehow a bad person who needs to become a good one, then you might as well use this book for something more useful like balancing a wobbling table, paper training a dog or teaching children fire safety. I mean it.

But if you are here because you see the potential to create and redeem with a higher regard for Life, then you've got the picture!

Re:LIFE is not a get-out-of-jail-free card.

Another danger is to believe that being Life-based means that mistakes or lack of performance does not matter. Some even have a false belief that a regard for Life means you can get away with doing nothing. This is really stretching Re:LIFE way out of context.

There is a little bit of a paradox here.

On one hand, to be Life-based means eliminating our expectations of good and accepting those who fall short into the Gap. When somebody fails to perform, having a regard for Life makes performance a nonissue. The real issue is how the situation can be redeemed for Life.

On the other hand, to have a regard for Life and yet to accomplish nothing means nothing beneficial is created and that all is futile. Re:LIFE really becomes just another dead touchy-feely idea if it doesn't lead us to achieve actual results. Maintaining a level of performance-based excellence allows the greater advancement of Life for all of us. This means performance is important.

How do we reconcile the two? We just have to accept that tension and balance will always be required. If we use Re:LIFE to provide freedom from performance-based pressures, we receive the benefit of being able to make mistakes and to learn from them. But this doesn't mean there shouldn't be consequences for lack of performance.

These consequences can be Life-based.

Not only am I a fan of the UFC but I am just as big of an NFL fan. (Go Vikings!) What I love about the game of football more than anything is the role of the coach when it comes to the dynamics of a team. I have observed some of the best coaches in the game understand the essence of Re:LIFE. Let me explain.

Some of the greatest coaches in professional sports understand the concept of Life-based consequences when building a team culture. Their goal is to motivate each player with Life within the team in contrast to the Gap of personal performance.

So what happens when, let's say, a quarterback of a football team fails to perform? Does he immediately have to clear out his locker and leave the club? No. Voting someone off the island is the typical Gap-based response. To a great football coach, the consequence for non-performance simply means that the player in concern receives less responsibility on the field. In most cases, it involves a support role where they are asked to help the other quarterbacks prepare during practice and succeed come game time. This is a Life-based consequence because it redeems the lack of performance into something positive that helps the team. The motivation to improve and accept more responsibility also creates a nice tension and balance between a culture of competitive improvement and teamwork.

The fact is Life has much more opportunity to advance when we perform to our potential. But we must avoid the trap of making that performance, or lack thereof, the point of motivation. Great performance is neither good nor bad. Great performance should be a by-product of Life-based motivation.

Re:LIFE is not becoming a doormat.

I've saved this one for last because it has the most potential danger to stifle Life before it even has a chance to transform us.

Throughout my brief stint as a junior high and high school teacher, I have met students who are always getting walked on by their peers. You probably know the type. These are the kids who do everybody else's homework in a sincere attempt to make friends, only to get their heads wrapped with duct tape like mummies who went down the wrong lane at the local home depot (true story!). And no matter how hard they try to be kind and generous, their reward is disrespect and more abuse.

In the professional world, owners of companies can fall into the same category. Some well-intentioned managers, in an attempt to retain the best people, can become generous to a fault. Overextending salaries and benefits and complying with every little request can actually have the opposite of the intended effect. An unhealthy culture of expectation is established, and it disenfranchises the entire organization.

The lesson here is that, without boundaries, we can quickly fall into the Gap. Any relationship that starts Life-based can become co-dependent and unfortunately abusive without the proper boundaries.

How do you know when you need boundaries?

Boundaries are necessary when the act of regarding Life for the sake of others extracts an unhealthy toll on your own well-being. This falls into the category of doing all the wrong things for the so-called right reasons. What may start with sincere Life-based intentions can quickly become a Gap-based nightmare that chips us away until there is nothing left but bitterness and resentment. And the worst possible result of a lack of boundaries is opening the door to and tolerating mental or even physical abuse.

Do you know anybody who has a hard time standing up for themselves? Do you know someone who seems to always agree to do things that they don't want to do or are unhealthy to begin with? How about people who agree to get walked all over in order to avoid conflict or become an easy target for those that edify themselves at the expense of others? Have you experienced any of the above? These are signs that Life-based boundaries are necessary.

Boundaries are for protection. You will not have the ability to regard Life in any creation or redemption capacity if you have no regard for the very Life within yourself! Protecting your personal time and energy are good examples of this. I myself was notorious for having very weak boundaries in this area as a pastor. I would burn all my time and energy on the spiritual needs and requests of others to the point of hurting my own family. What kind of an example was I setting giving advice to others when my very own world was crumbling?

Boundaries are also for the protection of others. Again, let's use my past role as a pastor as an example. If the inevitable result of being overcommitted and alienating my family was burnout, what do you think happened to the individuals who were depending upon me to deliver on my promises? People got hurt, and I had to take responsibility for my part of their false expectations. Had I understood the principle of Life-based boundaries earlier, I could have avoided a great deal of collateral damage to relationships and situations in the community.

Having a healthy regard for your own Life within you does not mean you are selfish. It means you are wise to the fact that we are human and have all the related limitations.

There is absolutely nothing wrong with setting boundaries and enforcing them. It is not okay to not defend yourself and consequently allow others to act out their own Gap-based behaviours. It is not okay to always avoid conflict just because you want to preserve peace at the expense of the Life in you. Yes, you may be called to tolerate or ignore certain Gap-based situations now and then, but only up to a certain point. When it means having disregard for Life, boundaries become an absolute necessity.

REFRAME: COMPARING THE GAP & LIFE

"Life is the art of drawing without an eraser."

—John W. Gardner

If this so far feels like you are drinking water from a firehouse, do not fret. While some people seem to have instantaneous aha light-bulb moments, it literally can take others up to several weeks or days to really understand Re:LIFE within the context of their personal lives. How quickly the seeds of Life germinate and sprout in our hearts is an individual and intensely personal experience. Life takes just the right time for everybody.

To add a little water to the seeds, let me try and make this as simple as possible and compare Gap and Life. But fair warning, sometimes the simplest things are the hardest to receive. This has to do with the fact that we, as a culture, pride ourselves on our intellect. We often like to believe that the more complicated we can make something, the more value it has (or the more important we look) when really, true genius and beauty is in simplification.

When tackling any type of concept, I like to ask others to explain things to me like I was a ten-year-old child. This immediately bypasses any assumptions or predispositions in either party for the sake of finding a path for clear communication. So let me do the same here for understanding Gap and Life.

Gap is all about anything *you* compare to being good or bad. It is all about *your* expectations and *your* judgments on *yourself* and the world around *you*. In other words, it is all about *you* and only has power if it can make it all about just that—*you*.

Life, on the other hand, is all about loving everything and anything outside of *you*. Life is all about submitting your desire to control what is good and bad and just accepting everything as an opportunity for creation and redemption. And the best part about Life is that if you allow yourself to walk in the highest aspiration and expression of love, then all your needs get taken care of because you will invite the same into your world.

Again, the Gap is about *you* – *your* needs, *your* desires, *your* standards, *your* hurts, and *your* expectations. The Gap is inwardly focused and makes *you* the point. *The Gap can never be fixed or filled because as a myth, it was never meant to exist in the first place.*

Life, on the other hand, takes you on an adventure of abundance by focusing outward and upward to new heights of your personal design and destiny. Life really teaches you about love despite the fact that nobody, including yourself, is perfect. You could say that Life really gives us the true freedom to live.

On the next page is a comparative breakdown of the difference between Gap and Life-based motivations. I always find it very helpful to see them side by side. I hope it is helpful for you too.

Motivation:	Gap	Life
Question:	Asks: How far is this from good, and how can I fix it?	Asks: How can I have a higher regard for Life?
Traits:	Filled with shame, doubt, fear, anxiety, anger, and insecurity.	Advancement of Life through creation and redemption.
Roots:	Knowledge of good and bad cause judgement.	The highest aspiration and expression of love.
The Reality:	The Gap can never be fixed or filled. Just reveals more of the Gap.	We do not need to be fixed as Life has nothing to do with good or bad.
Self-Image:	Always concerned with being good and not being a loser	The Gap is actually an opportunity for security and significance.
Performance:	Personal value, including relationships, is all performance-based.	Takes responsibility where possible with Life-based consequences.
Boundaries:	No boundaries that lead to codependency and other dysfunctions.	Healthy boundaries that protect and preserve Life within us.
Final Result:	Attracts and feeds other Gaps. Motivation fades.	Peace and freedom. Passion and purpose motivates.

RESPOND: THE GAP STRIKES BACK

"Life is like riding a bicycle. To keep your balance you must keep moving."

— Albert Einstein

By now, if you truly understand the difference between the seeds of motivation, you should have received the revelation that *we do not need to be fixed*. We are on the same page, fantastic, but I understand this has caused some interesting stress.

The fact that you don't need to be fixed might be a little strange to take. This was pointed out to me by Megan, the Re:LIFE leader whose personal story you read earlier. Megan once said to me bluntly, "Ed, we live in a society where everything and everyone needs to be fixed. It's actually stressful to hear that nothing's wrong with you."

At the risk of causing a little anxiety, I would like to affirm that *you do not need to be fixed.* Nothing is wrong with you! That's because when Re:LIFE wins, the Gap of where we fall short of good actually becomes an opportunity to build personal security and significance. When the Gap is no more, we actually reach a state where we are more at peace with ourselves and feel the freedom to pursue purpose and passion in Life.

But this doesn't mean the Gap is just going to surrender and lie down for a ten count. No way.

Think of the Gap as an ugly ravenous ogre that gets crankier and more demonstrative the less it gets fed. When you are constantly feeding the Gap and letting it motivate your thoughts and actions, it lays quiet and satiated. But when you refuse to give in and satisfy its desires, the inner conflict can actually intensify.

This is the bad news, and there is one really good reason for it. *Nothing worthy of true Life ever comes easy.* Think about this for a moment.

When a mother gives birth to a child, it is an extremely painful experience. Not only has she carried all that weight and discomfort for nine months, but the process of giving birth involves certain miraculous physiological logistics that I shudder to even fathom.

But all that sweat, blood, and tears set the stage for the true miracle made possible in Life. There is just something undeniably special in the bond between mother and child after months of oneness that culminate with hours of struggle in delivery. Re:LIFE has the same effect. The greater the Gap that is to be overcome, the sweeter and more appreciated Life is.

Beyond the intensification of the inner conflict, the Gap will also seem to become more subtle in its approach. Many times what may appear to be Life-based might actually be the Gap in disguise. This is a result of the subconscious preconditioning we receive from the world around us. The more you deal with the obvious Gaps, the deeper you will go to realize that there are even more Gap-based motivations hidden beneath the surface. So my next piece of bad news is that overcoming the Gap will be a life-long battle. Every stage of our journeys will reveal new levels of the Gap in different ways.

When I was in high school, I faced certain Gap-based issues. When I became a young single professional, a whole new set of Gap-based challenges arose in my life. And just as I had victory and freedom over those, I decided to get married, which just revealed more of the Gap within me than ever before. And I won't even begin to get into what happened to me when children were added to the mix!

For this reason, it's important to understand that being Gap-based and Life-based may look the same on the surface. They may both entail the same set of actions and results. But be wary! The single determining attribute that distinguishes a Gap-based person from a Life-based one is motivation. What may appear to be the right thing to do may be sabotaged because it is done for all the wrong reasons.

Again, motivation is all that matters. And having a Life-based motivation means reaching for the highest aspiration and expression of love. Love is the single determining factor. Without love, it doesn't matter how good everything looks because it all revolves around the Gap. Let's look at some examples of this.

For most, getting an education and finding a job is accepted as being smart and responsible. But what if the motivation behind a certain education and career choice is Gap-based? The result is people who are unhappy with their professional lives and who even begin resenting those that encouraged them into that position in the first place.

Several young men and women have approached me asking me for my opinion on their possible and carefully considered career paths. I ask them to share with me some of their prospective options. While I listen, if I detect even a little hint of indecisiveness, the next question I ask is why they made those specific choices. If their response is one of passion and pursuit of purpose, I know a Life-based decision has been made and everything will work out fine. But if they confess that they are trying to make their parents or spouses happy, or somehow they feel like their career will close the Gap of some type of social or financial status, I am quick to point out that their Gap-based motivations will inevitably cause great regret and dissatisfaction.

Can you see how something generally considered good can be twisted into something very, very bad? Here is another example of this using my family and how Re:LIFE applies to being a parent.

Let me start by sharing that when it comes to raising my sons Orlando and Julian, I put in great effort to strike out the term "good boy" from my vocabulary. As hard as it was at first, instead of saying "Good boy," when my son is obedient or does something positive, I simply say, "Thank you." I also refuse to reward my children for behavior that should be a healthy standard occurrence in my household.

Instead, I prefer to shower them with random acts of love, such as trips for ice cream, regardless of whether they are behaved or not. I never want my children to feel like they have to perform for my affection. My love is unconditional; however, I still discipline them to learn that the world is full of performance-based equations. I want them to know that to live in Life with full abundance, they need to understand certain lessons while they are young.

When my wife and I started having children, it brought me closer to my parents. I loved the fact that my mother and father had become grandparents. The problem occurs when my son's grandma, my mother, comes over and says, "Because you were such a good boy today, I'm going to buy you a present!" And sometimes, instead of a present, she resorts to rewards in cold, hard cash.

Even at the current tender age of four years, Orlando knows how to play the grandma game to get what he wants. He is more than happy to say and do all the right things in her presence with the knowledge that by his performance he will be rewarded.

Let me just say I have no problem with the prerogative every grandparent has to spoil their grandchildren. After the hell I put my parents through, I completely understand how adorable my two sons can be and how good it feels to lavish them with generosity. But when I see my son clutching a $20 bill and asking his grandma when they are going to the toy store, I shudder at the messages we are sending.

It all emotionally hits a little too close to home for comfort in my mind. This is because when I was growing up, I was controlled by my own Gap-based motivations of wanting the approval of my parents. I quickly learned that performance such as good grades and other academic accolades would induce an act of approval in my family. I wrongly assumed my parents only loved me when I performed to their standards. And so, when I fell short, I felt shame and fear.

This later evolved into a performance-based mentality where my personal worth was strictly based upon how good I was doing in areas such as career and status. It became the root for much of my personal burnout and people-pleasing behaviours in my adult years.

From my mother's perspective, she was doing all she could back then to be a good mother—just as she is now trying to be a good grandparent. Her Gap-based motivations are unmistakeably evident. I see this all the time. Unfortunately many parents have to face the temptation of living out our own Gaps vicariously through our children. The trap is that we can use our children's performance to make us feel better as good parents and thus experience a false sense of security and significance as a family.

Getting back to the situation with my mother and my son, how do I handle it? Do I point out my mother's Gap and make everyone feel bad about wanting to do all the right things for the wrong reasons? No. I love her and just couldn't do that.

My solution is to work with my wife to create a Life-based response to the gifts and cash offerings. This is why we have recently taken a portion of the children's toys and given them to an underprivileged family, with Orlando participating in the entire process. Orlando and I also discuss my choice of computer desktop image, which happens to be the same as the one on the cover of this book. I use the image to explain that some little boys don't have any toys or even regular meals, and it is our family's passion and purpose to help them.

This is an example of how I am doing all I can to use the Gap as an opportunity to build Life-based security and significance in myself and my family.

I am now going to show you step-by-step how to do the same.

RESPOND: THE FOUR-STEP METHOD TO LIFE

"Life loves to be taken by the lapel and told, 'I am with you kid. Let's go!'"

—Maya Angelou

By now, you have a full understanding of the difference between Gap-based and Life-based motivations. I hope I have clearly demonstrated the glaring difference between each regardless of their perceived similarities on the surface.

I am now going to teach you how to practically apply Re:LIFE into any situation of life in real time.

Becoming proficient at Re:LIFE is comparable to becoming a judo master. As with any martial arts or any physical discipline, at first this will feel clunky and awkward.

Also think of it like learning how to drive a car with standard transmission for the first time. Be prepared for some herky-jerky stop-and-go journey with a few stares from other drivers and pedestrians for good measure.

The point is practice makes perfect. Soon, Re:LIFE will become second nature. You will be driving down the road and judo flipping yourself happy in no time without even thinking about the mechanics involved.

Just always keep in mind that this is not about whether or not you are good at Re:LIFE. Many individuals I coach come to me discouraged thinking that since they know the strategy, they should be perfect at it.

Re:LIFE is about direction, not perfection.

So don't be discouraged if this takes a bit of time. Just get pointed in the right direction, and it will get easier and easier.

Re:LIFE can be implemented in any situation where a Gap occurs in an easy four-step process. You might notice that I have been actually using each step as a framework for this book. The steps are:

Recognize

Reframe

Respond

Reflect

Let's spend some time breaking down each step into an analysis of why it is important and an identification of the tangible actions we can take. Each step builds upon the other and gets more important. So, as tempting as it may be to jump ahead, please try to stay in order.

First step is to *recognize* the Gap.

Emotions such as shame or any of its cousins like fear, guilt, anxiety, or stress, in general, are the perfect triggers to begin recognizing the Gap. Other clear triggers include feeling judged, insecure, or angry. Sometimes these emotions physically manifest into behaviours like babbling, getting defensive, or confusion in thought and behaviour.

When you experience these emotions, don't judge them as good or bad. Instead, ask yourself, "Why am I feeling this way?" There is a good chance you are experiencing something that has fallen short of good, and into the Gap. In most cases, this involves some sort of expectation of something or someone—even an expectation on yourself. At this point, you are at a critical juncture between Gap and Life.

Recognizing the Gap at first can be a bit tough. We have been conditioned to just accept the Gap, and so this may seem like a very counterintuitive experience.

One of easiest ways I have found to recognize the Gap in my life is to look for signs of what I have been taught and come to understand it as the Drama Triangle. I make no claims of creating the Drama Triangle but have adapted it to Re:LIFE and continue to use it in all I do. The Drama Triangle consists of three distinct expressions of the Gap: persecutor, rescuer, and victim. The Drama Triangle is so called because in most dramatic situations, there are typically three main roles we can play. And although we may find ourselves in any role at any given time, I find that every person tends to default to two primary ones based on their personalities. Once again the three roles of the Drama Triangle are:

Persecutor

Rescuer

Victim

If you begin persecuting others in judgment and condemnation, it's a sign that you have fallen into Gap-based motivations. Persecutors tend to act self-righteous and are particularly frustrated by the fact that people just don't get it. Persecutors are often very legalistic and can be critical of not just others, but themselves.

Now if you find yourself trying to rescue the person or situation, especially when it is not your responsibility to begin with, then chances are you have become just as Gap-motivated as the persecutor. Rescuers tend to become overcommitted and start to feel taken for granted or resentful despite their best efforts to do the right thing.

Finally, the victim tends to become Gap-based by throwing a tantrum, blaming everybody and everything around them, and taking absolutely no responsibility for anything. Whether victims do anything externally or not, they are in complete rebellion. The interesting thing about the victim is that they have all the power and force the persecutor and rescuer have used on them.

What is also important to note about the victim is where the persecutor and rescuer can often recognize their own behaviours, the victim typically requires an external indicator to snap things into focus. Dr. Phil is particularly good at this; he does it by videotaping those who have entered into a victim mentality and exposing them during playback like a full-length mirror. Victims rarely welcome or even accept what they see in that mirror, but when they do, real change transformation is usually imminent.

The common trait between all three roles here is a tremendous sense of insecurity and insignificance. This involves questioning your own worth and a sense of helplessness. The shame behind insecurity and insignificance makes us withdraw as victims, go on the offense as persecutors, or just try harder as rescuers. The ultimate end result for all of them is a negative one.

Second step is to *reframe* the Gap with a higher regard for Life.

Now that you have recognized the Gap, "How can I make this about Life?" is the question you want to be asking at this juncture. Remember, Life is the greatest aspiration and expression of love, so love has to be part of the reframing process. Your goal is to find a different perspective that creates a newfound regard for Life in the situation.

The secret here is to take not just any perspective but an *external* one. Remember, no matter how big or small a problem may appear, when it is in your face, it completely blocks your peripheral view. This requires you to either find another source to provide a Life-based look, or to step out of yourself and pretend to be an objective third party.

A fantastic method commonly used to reframe is to place yourself in the other person's shoes, especially if the Gap involves some type of relational conflict. You can resort to the question, "How would I like to be treated in this situation?"

This is why peer-to-peer coaching is so important. In Re:LIFE, relationships are important because they provide that external perspective we often miss. My wife is my best friend and greatest Re:LIFE coach in the world. How so? We have worked out a wonderful system where she recognizes the moment I slip into a Drama Triangle role, which usually involves a combination of rescuer and persecutor. She then confronts me, which allows me to share any feelings of insecurity or insignificance. This then triggers her reframing skills, and I get all the healthy Life-based perspective I need.

Remember, making something about Life involves either the act of creation or redemption or many times a healthy dose of both. Every Gap is an opportunity to ask, "What can be created for the sake of Life here?" Or, "How can this be redeemed to Life?"

Third step is to *respond* by turning from the Gap to Life.

Once the Gap has been reframed, your job is to begin acting on the opportunity for the creation or redemption of Life, no matter how small the action may appear. Sometimes turning to Life may feel uncomfortable and may require sacrifice. This also might be a time to work out or enforce some boundaries.

There are some key responses that are needed to turn from the Gap to Life for each role in the Drama Triangle.

If you find yourself persecuting, your first response should be to seek and act out of empathy. During the reframe step, you should put yourself in their shoes to gain an understanding. Then you should respond in the same way you would want to be treated if you happened to be in the same situation.

If you tend to be the rescuer, as counterintuitive as it may sound, your immediate response should be to do *nothing*. The old adage of, "It's better to be harmless and not helpful," applies to you. Giving yourself that pause allows you to formulate the proper response even if it means to do nothing. To the rescuer, sometimes the best yet most excruciating thing to do is just let people hit the wall and deal with their own consequences. You can't always be the hero and shouldn't let Gap-based thinking dupe you into believing you need to save every situation or make everyone happy all the time.

Finally if you are a victim, your first response should be very simple and straightforward: just do something—and not just any old something but something that's not about you! For the victim, externally focused momentum is critical to cure the blame game and go from victim to victory.

Turning from the Gap to Life requires humility and sincerity. It's not just enough to be sorry for acting and reacting from Gap-based motivations. One must be willing to turn completely 180 degrees from the Gap to Life. This always requires thinking less one ourselves and being true to the Life that calls out to all of us!

The fourth and final step is to *reflect* on the results.

The act of reflection is a calm, lengthy, and intent consideration of a situation or experience. This type of reflection leads to retention, reinforcement, and refinement.

The more you honestly reflect, the more you will retain the process of Re:LIFE for next time. And the more you retain, the more you will positively reinforce the principles of Re:LIFE in everything you do. Finally, the more positive reinforcement you experience, the more you can refine the process to be even more effective.

Authentic reflection is a highly underrated skill in any personal-development repertoire. But reflection is the currency used to build up a valuable portfolio of wisdom.

Warning: there is no such thing as an *instant* result.

Sometimes it takes me a good week to even months to apply this four-step process and win the internal battle between Gap and Life. Remember, Gap can be very deceptive, and you will never eliminate it completely. The more entrenched the Myth of Motivation deception, the longer it will take to recognize the Gap and turn from it to Life. Let me share an example of my experience of working as a teacher.

The industry of education, for the most part, is completely Gap-based. The concept of keeping grades as the scorecard does nothing but create Gap-motivated students who start their adulthood believing that good grades mean a good degree, which ultimately means a good career and life. Schools, although as institutions are well intentioned, are notorious for spreading the Myth of Motivation.

Inevitably, most realize that their perfectly planned career and paths to self-fulfillment are not as straight and paved with gold as one is led to believe. In many ways, focusing on good grades often creates a false sense of entitlement. This is where a student who received an MBA with honors believes he or she should secure a six-figure salary as an executive the day after graduation. But every CEO and HR manager will tell you, it takes more than good grades to really be considered an asset in the corporate environment — or any arena of life in general.

While there are schools that are trying to break this paradigm, teachers in general, because of their own conditioning, default to Gap-based tactics to increase performance in their classes. I was no different when I first started teaching.

As a teacher, it took me an entire five months struggling with the behavior and lack of performance of certain students before I recognized how Gap-based my motivation for teaching was. I would go to bed at night just thinking I was a bad instructor, and my own Gaps would keep getting bigger and bigger. I would bounce from persecutor — getting completely aggravated by students who just didn't gel with my program — and rescuer — thinking I just had to work harder and become their best friend in order to see the results I was looking for.

Then one day, I decided to reframe the whole situation. I stepped back and asked myself what I would have wanted from my teachers back when I was a student. And after multiple conversations with some great peer coaches in my life, I just accepted that there are more important priorities than good grades and good students. Instead of trying to look like a good teacher for my superiors, I decided to focus on creating a process for learning that would really advance Life in each young adult that signed up for my class.

The results were amazing. I considered some of the most at-risk students my pals, and we shared a much deeper connection than just an academic one. I even taught a student version of *Re:LIFE* that impacted fellow teachers who worked in my program.

I would still implement class discipline for falling short of performance benchmarks — especially the ones we all agreed upon together. But I approached it all from a Life perspective. I would have conversations with some of the toughest kids on how their actions were affecting their ability to really experience Life. I openly shared how I was continually going from Gap to Life through personal stories and metaphors from movies.

Some students responded well, while others didn't. But none of that mattered anymore. There was no more judgment. No Gap. Just Life. After that shift to Life, something amazing occurred.

I began to really love being a teacher.

Don't get me wrong. There were still days that I wanted to leap from my desk across the room and in one swooping manoeuvre decapitate the heads of half the class with a ruler. That's where my internal conflict between Gap and Life continued to wage.

Thankfully when it comes to teaching, it's been getting easier and easier to recognize, reframe, and quickly respond to any Gap deception. I reflect upon the results constantly, and this allows me to refine my teaching methods. Not only has it made me a better professional teacher, but I have benefited in every situation where I have been called to educate or train others. This includes training and mentoring as a company manager and father.

To top it all off, I experienced the sweetest victory of them all when I took one of my classes out for burger and milkshakes followed by a night by a campfire on the final day of their final exams. I had spent years working with this group of teens, and now they were practically adults graduating from high school. The payoff came when they thanked me and actually requested an ongoing relationship because of all the Re:LIFE coaching they had received. By finding harmony between results and relationships, many of these former students have now become part of my spiritual family. I am proud to mentor them and be considered an integral part of their success in the future.

I hope this inspires you to do the same in every opportunity for Re:LIFE. Remember, it's not always going to be *easy*, but it will definitely be *worth it*.

Are you ready to begin applying the four steps of Re:LIFE to your current situations? Go ahead and try it. Here are the steps again to try in your own situations:

Step 1:

Recognize **the Gap.**

Step 2:

Reframe **the Gap with a higher regard for Life.**

Step 3:

Respond **by turning from the Gap to Life.**

Step 4:

Reflect **on the results.**

REFLECT: THREE CIRCLES OF RE:LIFE

"Life is much more manageable when thought of as a scavenger hunt as opposed to a surprise party."

—Jimmy Buffet

While writing, I have been reflecting on some of the results of using Re:LIFE to help others for the past few months.

Through my reflections, I have noticed a problem starting to occur. It's actually a great problem to have. I've chosen to turn this problem into an opportunity, or what can be called a "probletunity."

The problem is that everywhere I turn, more people are receiving the gift of Re:LIFE. Just yesterday I had coffee with an old acquaintance from my pastoral days, and what I thought would be a quick sixty-minute catch-up chat turned into a two-and-a-half hour Re:LIFE celebration! And this suits me just fine when I see the aha moments and the light bulbs of freedom go off in their eyes.

The crux of the problem, however, is that those of us who receive the gift of Re:LIFE instinctively seek a supporting community of practice, where they can begin applying Re:LIFE into their lives in a safe environment. "Re:LIFErs" actually want to live Life together!

So I began exploring different structures from other successful Life-based communities. I reflected on what worked and didn't work for me in the past. What I have come up with is an amalgamation of personal experience and great advice from other community leaders.

I share this here because not everybody who reads this and receives the gift of Re:LIFE will actually be in my immediate sphere of relational contact. Nor is that necessarily the healthiest thing because it might become all about me and not Life. Besides, my dream is to see Re:LIFE go global into every community possible. So there had to be a way to cross cultural and geographical boundaries and let Life advance wherever it may.

There is a group of us who have been living and modelling Re:LIFE together. I will share with you what we do, and if you feel empowered and compelled to do the same, have a go at it! I claim nothing in Re:LIFE as my own because it is based upon spiritual principles that have been around far longer than I have. Although the name "Re:LIFE" is original and belongs to me, everything else is public domain and fair game as long as it is used for the purposes of Life.

Those that enter into a relationship with our group of Re:LIFErs are invited into what I call a Re:LIFE village. Within this village, we all at some point make a commitment to holistically live out the three circles of Re:LIFE. Before I explain this further, let me share why I feel this is absolutely critical and needed in today's culture.

There is a behavioral condition that is affecting a growing number of people in North American culture. It is an unprecedented phenomenon of group isolation—what author Randy Frazee calls "Crowded Loneliness" in his book *Making Room for Life* (a fitting title for what this is all about, don't you think?).

Crowded Loneliness is a symptom of what I call Relational Poverty. It is a condition that stems from our desire to live in Life with purpose and passion in the context of meaningful relationships. It occurs when we feel alone in our pursuit of Life, or when nobody seems to relate to us because everyone is too preoccupied doing their own thing. Crowded Loneliness is extremely deceptive because it just does not make sense why we feel so unfulfilled and lost when we seem surrounded by so many opportunities for connecting with others.

You may or may not be experiencing Crowded Loneliness. But in my experience, almost everyone who is interested in Re:LIFE, experiences it in some way or other. For those who understand the effects of this cultural condition, let me share with you the systemic cause of the issue. The roots of Crowded Loneliness can be found in how we compartmentalize and integrate Life into our worlds on a daily basis.

Everyone knows the story of the Titanic. It was built to be an unsinkable ship. The reason its creators made such a bold claim is that several water-tight compartments were built into the hull of the boat. This meant that if one compartment was flooded, the others would stay water-free and keep the boat afloat. However, there was one major flaw, and it had nothing to do with the design but with how the hull was put together.

In 2006, new evidence emerged from an expe-riment by two metallurgists, Tim Foecke, of the US National Institute of Standards and Technology, and Jennifer Hooper McCarty, of Oregon Health and Science University. Foecke and Hooper were able to scientifically prove that the liner would have survived the collision long enough for most of, or even all, its passengers to be rescued had it not been put together with weak rivets. According to their research, it was these rivets that caused the Titanic's hull to unzip on impact with the ice.

This is the perfect metaphor for a major mistake that people make when pursuing healthy and successful lives. We have all the right ideas and get the design right, but the way all the pieces are integrated together is not strong enough to withstand the collisions. So our lives unzip, and the flood eventually turns into a tragic catastrophe like the one that inspired the hit movie.

Can you think of a time when your life unzipped and flooded? I can think of a few in my life, and none of them are pretty.

To prevent this from happening and ensure we have the best chance to find security and significance through purpose and passion, we must integrate Life into everything we do. The highest regard for Life acts as strong rivets that make everything hold together amidst any challenge.

Our community has identified three main areas that we need to experience in Life, to practically integrate Re:LIFE into our day-to-day existence. These are the three circles of Re:LIFE:

Compassion

Community

Communion

Let's examine each in more detail.

Compassion is how much we can *receive* and *reciprocate* unconditional love.

A life of compassion is critical, but unfortunately, there seems so little compassion that is unconditional. Whenever someone extends an unsolicited gift or act of kindness, we have been conditioned to ask, "What's the catch?"

Materialism is also another huge challenge to compassion. We cannot let this deter us from integrating compassion into our lives. The Bible says, "Where your treasure is, there will your heart be also." I think this is an extremely effective evaluation method to see where our hearts really are. If our heart motivations are Life-based, our treasures will follow suit. But if we are Gap-based, our treasures will mostly be spent on ourselves.

To expand this concept a bit further, treasure does not necessarily mean money. Often the most valuable treasures we can extend are our time and talents. In some cases, time is the real treasure. If you asked my wife if she would rather have piles of cash from me instead of family time, she would take the latter any day. On other occasions, I have spent time making paintings for my business associates that are much more valued than any financial gift I could afford. My good friend Donnie still brings up the topic of a blue horse he asked me to paint for him on a business trip to Texas. He, like many others, appreciates a gift of talent more than finances because of the time and energy it takes to paint a picture. It is a gift that I was proud to share.

In the Re:LIFE village, we try to express compassion in the following ways:

Benevolent Actions

Spontaneous Blessing

Sacrificial Giving

Encouragement and Coaching

Encouragement and coaching is usually the first and easiest act of compassion to give and receive. Encouragement is like fertilizer when it comes to the soil of hearts. We try to encourage everybody to participate in peer coaching when it comes to putting Re:LIFE into practice.

Past compassion activities have included volunteering and getting together for Impact Kitchens. This is where we all experience a small cooking lesson and then cook meals for those less fortunate. My wife has found her passion in helping immigrant wives and mothers explore and experience Canadian culture. Some of our Re:LIFE villagers are championing massive projects, such as working with former convicts transitioning back into society and providing guide dogs for physically disadvantaged and underprivileged children.

Everywhere we go, there is an opportunity to live out the circle of compassion. One just has to be looking upward and outward instead of downward and inward. The circle of compassion is only limited by our motives and creativity!

If you want to truly live Re:LIFE, acts of compassion are the perfect way to focus on Life and not the Gap.

When was a time when you felt compassion and acted on it? How did it feel? When was the last time you received an act of compassion? How did that feel?

Community is our sense of *identity* in the context of *meaningful relationships.*

Whether we like it or not, we are all part of a community. The real question is how much is that community a part of you? Our identity is defined by who we are associated with. If we live in Canada, we are Canadians alongside those around us. If we work for a company, we are identified by the department or hierarchy in relation to fellow employees. It is unavoidable.

In Re:LIFE, we build community by the act of sharing.

For example, there is something simply beautiful in the act of sharing a meal when building relationships. Eating and gathering culturally and relationally is a very intimate experience. In many cultures, to share a meal together is a highly regarded expression of friendship, respect, and love.

Unfortunately the temptation to isolate oneself and be individualistic prevents this type of sharing from happening. We are adopting a more individualistic culture every day. As a school teacher, I saw individualism more than ever. An increasing number of students can be found buried in earphones connected to iPods while scanning their laptops for the next great Youtube video.

When I was growing up, all the kids in the neighbourhood would gather in the streets for epic water fights, street hockey games, and Frisbee football. My street is eerily quiet today because of individualism and general distrust for neighbours.

Even as adults, individualism truly infringes upon our ability to work together and build strong communities that share common values. This is something I have traditionally struggled to find, and my participation in the Re:LIFE village acts as an important reminder of the power of a sharing community.

Together, we try to express the circle of community in the following ways. I think the ways speak for themselves:

Sharing Friends

Sharing Food

Sharing Experiences

Apprenticeship

Think of a time when you really felt part of a community that built and shared together. What were the qualities and activities of this community?

Communion is the *oneness* we feel in *body, mind,* and *spirit.*

By the term "communion," I am not implying any sort of institutional religious organization or structure. Some relate the term communion to what is commonly practiced in Catholic churches with wine and bread. Not that there is anything wrong with this traditional spiritual practice. I enjoy that sort of communion very much when appropriate.

You may or may not practice a personal faith-based belief system, and, if you do, I encourage you to continue to do so. I just make this distinction because I've found that religion for most people really creates a feeling of exclusivity, and this can kill a circle of community. We believe the best communities are meant to be Life-based and inclusive.

Communion, for me, means oneness between body, mind, and spirit. In my experience, being in a state of communion solves a lot of personal problems.

I believe stress is the result of a misalignment between our actions, thoughts, and hearts—body, mind, and spirit. It's like driving a car with all the wheels out of alignment. Eventually that car grinds itself to a halt. Stress, if unchecked, does exactly the same thing in our lives. The circle of communion is the answer to this problem.

When our actions (body), thoughts (mind), and our hearts (spirit) are all moving in one intentional direction, we experience a sense of purpose and peace. It is a feeling that transcends anything happening in our daily lives and uplifts the essence of our true being in exciting ways.

We are in communion with each other and the world around us when we feel free to share our values and beliefs. We are in communion when we give each other permission to explore and discover a life that is beyond our own physical needs or desires. Some call this faith; others call it spirituality. Some choose an organized religion to express communion, while others prefer less structure. Whatever the choice, communion is a critical part of our lives for that peace and encouragement.

What kills communion more than anything is consumerism. This is very similar to the condition of physical obesity. We can actually become emotionally and spiritually obese through consumerism. This happens when we just carry on consuming information and experience and yet put nothing into practice because we just think of ourselves as the buyers. Common health sense will tell you, the more caloric intake you ingest, the more is converted into fat and the body eventually becomes so sedentary that even if one wants to exercise, it is physically impossible to do so. The very same thing happens when consumerism prevents actual and practical application of emotional and spiritual knowledge.

I hate to say it, but this is what disheartened me about standing in front of a church every Sunday and talking about a spiritual life we were meant to live while everyone nodded in agreement. The congregation would tell me how great my sermons were only to go back to their regular lives unchanged. As I stated earlier, I still believe the church is beautiful in its original purpose. But it can be mistakenly confused with actual spiritual exercise and life application. If anything, church should be what happens after you leave the building and put those calories into good use!

In short, communion is not a spectator sport. Communion is fully participatory and is meant to be explored to its fullest.

In a Re:LIFE village, we try to model communion in the following forms:

Sharing Truth

Sharing Rest

Sharing Pain

Leadership

Communion happens when we sit and share with each other universal truths—especially the ones we have discovered that seem to always be constant regardless of how we feel. When we walk down the beach together making small talk just to rest and restore our energy and remind ourselves how sensational all of creation is—that's communion. And when we just sit in silence because someone in our community has lost a loved one, or listen to each other discussing some crisis over a late night cup of java, you have communion again. And when you are in bed at night reflecting on your day and introspectively celebrating how awesome Life can be ...

That's right, it's communion once again.

What does leadership have to do with communion? To me, leadership is the ultimate state of communion. Leadership requires our actions, thoughts, and hearts to be aligned for the purpose of advancing Life. You can't be a truly effective leader and not be in communion. Communion creates leadership, and lea-dership creates the opportunity for communion.

So when was your last experience of communion according to our definition of oneness of body, mind and spirit?

Does this all sound good to you? For me, nothing has been more inspirational and encouraging. But don't just take my word for it. Here is what some of the members of our Re:LIFE village are saying about how we have chosen to pursue Life together in the context of community:

> "I encourage everyone who is looking to some direction in their life to join [the village]. You will feel at ease to open up and learn some great techniques for taking charge of your life. The group is very supportive and would be beneficial for anyone at any stage in their life."

> "If you are open-minded, honest, and looking for a spiritual-based group to help facilitate personal growth in a casual, nonjudgmental environment, then this is the group for you."

> "Hi, Ed. Thank you *so* much. Your vision to change the world one person at a time is beyond inspiring. Your passion for this is contagious, and I'm excited to be involved in Re:LIFE at the grassroots level."

Don't be discouraged if you feel like one of the three circles of Re:LIFE is anaemic or is missing for you completely. I got great news for you.

When I was in elementary school, I used to watch an animated cartoon series called *GI-Joe*. My favorite childhood cartoon was just released as a live Hollywood blockbuster. At the end of every episode, the heroes would give a piece of advice. And each episode would end with the same cheesy-yet-fitting tagline that I leave with you now as an encouragement: "Now you know, and knowing is half the battle!"

So, now, for the sake of Life, let's fight the other half of the battle. Take action! Join a Re:LIFE village, or better yet, start one of your own!

REFLECT: RE:LIFE RE:LATIONAL

"No love, no friendship can cross the path of our destiny without leaving some mark on it forever."

—François Mauriac

I am going to take a few minutes to talk about relationships—especially relationships in the areas of romance and marriage. I actually wasn't intending to include this chapter, but after discussing Re:LIFE with our growing village, I think this is a great opportunity to shed some light on a really big issue I have identified in our North American culture.

Whether we like it or not, relationships affect us all. It is fair to say that any problem we have in our lives really boils down to some sort of breakdown in relationships. Whether it is a relationship with ourselves, friends, family, work associates, or the world around us, you cannot escape the effects of healthy or unhealthy relationships.

Many health experts say that preventative habits and lifestyle are far more effective than reactionary medicine and treatment. It's the same with relationships. We have the choice spend time reacting to issues rooted in relational brokenness, or we can spend it preventing the cause of it all. I prefer the latter because it allows us to concentrate on making the most of every opportunity both personally and professionally as against blowing our potential in Life through a constant state of insecurity.

This brings me to a massive issue I have recognized.

I've mentioned before that, as a whole, we, as a culture, are suffering from symptoms that stem from relational poverty. Relational poverty is exactly like financial poverty. When one doesn't have a healthy and well-managed source of income, our lives fall into jeopardy. The same is true for relational poverty. If one doesn't have healthy relationships, our personal happiness and ability to productively engage with the world is greatly at risk.

Relational poverty is a Gap that is killing us.

I think if everyone took a close hard look, we would all agree that romantic relationships today are far more complicated than they ever were. The typical tale of boy meets girl; boy likes girl; girl likes boy; boy and girl get married and live happily ever after; is pretty much gone the way of the dinosaur.

Today, between all the standard boy-and-girl stuff, you can throw in unplanned pregnancies, sexually transmitted diseases, infidelity, divorce, custody battles, and regular trips to the *Jerry Springer Show*. All these are signs of relational poverty.

Why is this happening?

It's simple. When we approach any form of relationship from a Gap-based motivation, we risk falling into relational poverty. This is what happens when single guys and girls date while they feel like something is wrong with them if they are not in some type of fairytale romance. This is what happens when a husband and wife decide to get a divorce because they are too busy thinking about how unfulfilled they are when everything was supposed to end happily ever after. This is what happens when any relationship starts to disintegrate because the Gap leads to challenges.

I have news that probably will not shock you: *relationships are hard work.* They take up a lot of time, space, and mental resources to keep happy and healthy.

Re:LIFE & The Myth of Motivation

In my opinion, no other show exemplified the challenges of relational poverty more than *Sex and the City*. It was a hit cable network dramatic comedy that examined the lives of four women struggling to find love and happiness amidst throngs of dysfunctional and desperate people. I think the reason the show was so popular because everyone could relate to it. The writers of *Sex and the City* weren't afraid to say what everybody was thinking. Every episode was about one relational Gap or another.

I hate to say it, but there is so much relational poverty around that a new show could be called "Sex and the *Inner* City." For all the surface glitz and glamour, the relational Gaps are just getting bigger and bigger.

We need to recognize these Gaps and turn from them back into Life-based relationships.

If the motivation for dating is the fear of being single and of being considered a loser, then every guy and girl out there better prepare themselves to drastically lower their standards. Out of this fear, one resorts to grab anybody with a pulse in an attempt to fix and fill their Gap. Tragedy happens in that we become more enamoured with dating the *idea* of a person and the Gap he or she fills, rather than loving the actual person for the sake of Life.

Dating is actually meant to be the process in which people are able to explore the purpose of Life together. This inevitably includes periods of heartbreak and singleness. What we consider bad about dating is actually an opportunity to learn and grow in Life.

And if irreconcilable differences were actually valid excuses for divorce, those that are married should all call it quits. The fact is, irreconcilable differences are just part of the territory and should not be taken as a Gap. One of the first couples that mentored my wife and me in marriage told us that if they knew *then* what they know *now* about each other, they never would have gotten married. But these differences gave them the opportunity to look past the faults and get down to the real nitty-gritty of being married.

Men and woman are designed different, so we can actually demonstrate true Life-based love and respect for one another that transcend imperfections. Sticking together with someone despite their Gap is what love is all about!

Not only are relationships hard work, they can be messy, inconvenient, and just plain intrusive. Why? Because having a regard for Life can be messy, inconvenient, and intrusive. And there is absolutely nothing wrong with that!

I once read a marvellous book that described marriage and any worthwhile relationship like a big tree growing in the middle of your house. The tree branches into every room and stretches its twigs and leaves into every nook and cranny it pleases. Is this messy, inconvenient, and intrusive? Absolutely!

But without the tree, is there really any Life in that home? Regardless of how perfect the house may be, its whole purpose is sadly wasted if there is no Life inside.

My wife and I often are afraid what people think when they come to our house. With our children currently almost five and two years old, it doesn't matter how much you pick up, clean, vacuum or scrub; in twenty minutes, the kids will systematically revert everything back to chaos. And I must admit, being a messy person myself, I really don't do much to help the situation. But who has time to keep a perfect house when you are busy building forts, playing human dog pile, and throwing each other across the room into a stack of cushions on the couch?

We felt that the insecurity of our chaotic home was being seen as a Gap in our parenting and housekeeping skills. This was until a realtor came by and shared with me something special. He said, "Ed, a perfectly clean home is a sign of unhappy and neglected children." And it made total sense. When you are busy living in Life, things get messy, and that's perfectly fine.

True Re:LIFE-based relationships will seriously mess things up for you. But when you really have a regard for Life, it's not all about you anymore, is it? Once we get over constantly focusing on the Gap within ourselves and others, relationships become easy. This is because when made a priority, Life just naturally grows and changes us into the fullness of our destinies.

This is why I love doing premarital coaching. Nothing is more rewarding than blowing away the fairy tale picture common to newly engaged couples. The sort of dazed shock on most men and women's faces when I tell them how messy their marriages will be because neither of them is perfect gives me the giggles.

But the real payoff occurs when I inform them that even though they will constantly fall short of the ideals of good husbands or wives, there is nothing to fix. The mere notion of fixing ourselves or others means the entire relationship is Gap-based. Instead of focusing on each other's Gaps, I encourage couples to bend over backward to make it about Life with their soon-to-be spouses. I explain that if all they did was make it about how to create and redeem with a regard for Life, then our own needs are naturally taken care of.

This message is both encouraging and relieving for most—especially in a culture where every relationship falls short and needs to be fixed. And this doesn't apply to just marriage.

Every relationship is worth a Life-based approach and makeover

We're all designed to be in happy and healthy relationships.

Is it time for you to get out of relational poverty? Here's your chance. Choose Life!

Do you feel you are suffering from relational poverty? How so?

REFLECT: RE:LIFE FINANCIAL

"In the book of life, the answers aren't in the back."

—Charles M. Schulz
(Charlie Brown speaking)

Is there a gap in your finances? Most would say yes. Re:LIFE applies to the way we approach finances as well. It may even be one of the most important applications because there are few forces in this world as powerful as money.

Just like everything else in Re:LIFE, when it comes to money, motivation matters. Some say money is the root of all evil. This is untrue. It is actually the *love* of money that causes our downfall. Failure to understand this causes many people to approach their finances from a Gap-based motivation.

We fall into the trap of loving money because we believe money can fix or fill the Gap in our lives.

On one hand, we believe that money will fix our insecurities because our society sells us a false bill of goods that claims material possessions will increase your status and protect us from rejection. Unfortunately in many cases this is true in a twisted sort of way because there are those in the world that will be your best friend if you have money.

On the other hand, we also believe that financial freedom will create an ability to pursue a greater life of significance. Independent wealth allows us to explore our passions and make a difference. This is true; however it often comes at a price that too often exceeds the benefit. Those that say, "I'll make a difference after I achieve wealth," and, "I'll have lots of time to pursue my passions after I get to the top of the corporate ladder," rarely get there. Even if they make it, they often find themselves too addicted to chasing short-term Gap-based gratification rather than staying true to their original intentions.

Money will never fulfill the Gap or provide true security or significance. Money was never meant to. Money has the potential to be either a powerful Life-giving force in the world around you, or a Gap-based seed of destruction. What money becomes to you is completely up to your motivation behind your relationship with it. Money is neither good nor bad; it is the personal motivation behind it that makes the distinction.

When we approach money from a Gap-based motivation, we will never have enough money. We will love money and loathe not having any money at the same time. Money will become the focus at the cost of Life.

People who are Gap-based when it comes to finances tend to use money to keep score. Money is a terrible way to keep score in terms of living successful lives. There are plenty of amazing examples of successful individuals whom we admire for their accomplishments and contributions to humanity outside of making money.

The other problem with having a Gap-based view of money is that we become fearful of what that Gap reveals in our lives. If you make less salary than the person next to you, what is it saying about you? The Gap is revealed in stark reality. We feel inadequate and then avoid taking a healthy responsibility for our finances. What happens next is we look to the wrong sources of money to give us a false sense that there is no Gap. This is when people overspend, go into bad debt, and live off credit cards because they fear facing their financial reality. This is a weakness I personally have had to overcome.

There is a Life-based approach to money. And that is to see how money can be used as a tool to advance Life. If saving, investing, and spending decisions are made from a Life-based motivation, then the amount of money one has at his or her disposal doesn't become an issue.

When my wife and I get stressed about our financial situation because we are reminded about the Gap concerning how much money we feel we should have, we try and take a Life approach. We ask ourselves, what we can do to advance Life with the money we have. And sometimes the solution has nothing to do with money at all; rather we use other forms of currency such as time and service. When I feel a pinch in my wallet, I try and become generous with my time, which always takes my focus off the Gap in my finances. My wife also finds ways to express Life through acts of service and kindness toward women in her community. It's amazing what can be done when how we see money gets reframed from a Life instead of a Gap perspective.

Don't get me wrong here. Money is important. I am not denying that. The reality is money is a necessary currency to make things happen. The fact that my finances have allowed me to even have the resources to create and share Re:LIFE is evidence that money does make certain things easier.

Steve Casey, of the Goliath Group, and I have to deal with the necessity of money every day. Steve understands how to be Life-based when it comes to money. We sit on a regular basis and dream about all the ways we could impact the world through our group of companies. But the more we dream, the more the reality sinks in that we need to be diligent about the financial realities of it all. Changing the world takes money! So we don't judge money or people who have very little or an abundance of it. We just accept that this is how the world works and then do our best to be examples of how Life is always more important than money.

This is why if you really are serious about having a Life-based approach to personal finances, you cannot be negligent with money. Money itself is neutral. It is the motivation behind the management and use of money that makes the difference.

My wife has taught me some hard lessons about the pitfalls of being negligent with money. There have been times when my choices with how I managed my family's money demonstrated a complete lack of regard or love for my wife and children. It was not like I was out gambling it all away or spending it on big toys. But it was in the area of the little things, such as saving when we can and having a healthy plan for the future, that I had fallen short.

I have now taken it upon myself to be as educated as possible about the financial industry, and I strongly recommend anybody reading this to do the same. I'm not talking about following the stocks or becoming an expert in Wall Street. What I mean is getting educated on financial issues like insurance, retirement planning, credit, and debt management. I have found that the more I learn, the easier it is to make Life-based decisions concerning finances.

So if you feel like there is a Gap in your financial situation, don't be discouraged. At this very time, the entire world is going through a financial crisis, and everybody is affected in some way or another. But this is why understanding the difference between Gap and Life-based financial management is more important than ever. It's when Gap-based decisions are made that we end up with the ramifications we are experiencing today.

Whether the economy is up or down, it will never affect you outside of just a bunch of changing numbers if you have a Life-based perspective on finances.

In what financial areas of your life are you experiencing the Gap? How can you transform them into Life-based motivations?

REFLECT: LIFE IN LOCKDOWN

"Life is no 'brief candle' to me. It is sort of a splendid torch which I have got hold of for the moment, and I want to make it burn as rightly as possible before handing it on to future generations."

—George Bernard Shaw

It was April of 2009, and I was going to prison in Nicaragua on the tenth day of our journey of compassion—no, not for the reasons one might expect.

Our team was scheduled to provide a healthy meal and other activities for 1,050 prisoners living in a facility built for 500. On this day, every inmate would receive the equivalent of gourmet catering in the form of chicken stew, rice, vegetables, and other vitamin-packed nutrients. This would be a welcome break from their regular sustenance of beans and rice.

Before serving lunch, we were escorted into a plain room filled with roughly one hundred chairs, a stage, and podium; there were bars on every window. Our team of twenty or so men and women sat down near the stage, not knowing what to expect.

To be honest, I suddenly got a fright when a barred door opened and approximately a hundred inmates began piling into the rows of white plastic chairs. The reality that we were in a room full of convicted criminals quickly sunk in for all of us. For better or for worse, I noticed one guard in the corner armed with only a black baton and staring solemnly forward; he didn't seem the least interested in the proceedings before him.

A prison chaplain stood up and addressed the crowd. Apparently there was a chaplaincy time scheduled. I simply sat there, hundreds of thoughts racing through my mind, as I scanned every face in the crowd and tried to imagine what life in confinement would be like. Many of the men were so young! I couldn't help but think of some of the youth I knew back home that might be headed down the same path.

Just as I was getting comfortable and thinking to myself, "This isn't so bad," one of our leaders, Jim, kneeled over behind me and whispered in my ear. What he said put a lump in my throat the size of a tennis ball, and I felt like a bucket of ice water was poured down my back in spite of the topical heat we were in.

"Ed, we felt like you were supposed to say something ... What do you think?" were Jim's words from what I could remember in my state of panic.

Have you ever had one of those moments when you just wish you could vanish into thin air, or wished a large metal object would randomly fly through the area and knock you unconscious, and yet you just know you are in the right place at the right time? I have them once in a while, and it is always accompanied by that little voice in your heart that nudges you and says, "You're ready for this ... Go on; take a risk."

So there I was, standing in front of a hundred prisoners. A microphone was put into my ever-so-slightly trembling hands, and Chico, my translator, gave me a huge grin.

As I looked into the faces of the crowd, I had a pure moment of clarity. In an instant, I understood the pain these men were experiencing; they were all judged and condemned for the Gaps in their lives. Calmness came over me, and after briefly clearing my throat, I began to speak.

"I just want to start by saying that none of you are any different than me. No matter what you have done, I am just as capable as you of doing the same. In fact, you are in many ways lucky because now the light is shining on you and you have nowhere to hide; there are many who appear free and yet are trapped in darkness. At this moment, I do not see you as prisoners who have been convicted of crime. I see you all as men. And I am here to give you a message of hope and true freedom in Life."

Of course the above, now that it has been written out and edited a few dozen times, sounds like I am the perfect improvisational public speaker. You can be sure I fumbled around with my words while my translator Chico made me sound like a superstar. But you get my drift. The point is, I was given an opportunity to create and redeem for Life—and there was no way I was going to squander it.

What was supposed to be a thirty-minute session turned into a three-hour one; it was one of the best experiences I ever had. I was privileged to listen to the stories of some of the men as all our male team members began dispersing through the room to connect in profound and spiritual ways. By the time the session was over, every man in that room lined up to shake my hand and look me in the eye with a gesture of thanks. I wished I could have known how to say in Spanish that they had more of an effect on me that day than I ever could have had on them.

In that prison, I had experienced the full power of Re:LIFE. The stage was then set for what would happen to me that very evening.

REFLECT: THE RE:LIFE RESPONSIBILITY

> "Happiness is as a butterfly which, when pursued, is always beyond our grasp, but which if you will sit down quietly, may alight upon you."

—Nathaniel Hawthorne

On the tenth day of any trip away from my family, I have an emotional breakdown.

I've learnt this little quirk about myself the hard way. When I am away from my family for exactly ten days, I begin to get homesick and negative. So imagine combining my homesickness with being thousands of miles away in Nicaragua amidst the worst conditions of poverty and injustice I had ever seen.

This is what brought me to the train wreck I described in the introduction. That very night I decided to take a moment to just sit quietly in the emptiness of both my hotel room and my heart. After several moments, I opened up my notebook and scrawled the beginnings of what you hold in your hand. It that stillness, what I discovered was my opportunity to let Life redeem me and to create something new.

Why do I share my Nicaraguan addictions meltdown and detox with you at the risk of sounding like a total fraud who can't keep his own life together, let alone help anybody else?

The answer is simple: being open with my weaknesses prevents pride. And pride is the single biggest killer of Re:LIFE.

Pride is like Kryptonite to Superman. It exposes our weaknesses and allows Gap-based motivations to consume our lives and eventually destroy us from the inside out. Pride leads to hypocrisy.

The answer to pride is transparency.

I am transparent with my weaknesses, so nobody, especially the ones that receive my help, ever gets the wrong idea about who I am or what I have to deal with. I am aware of my responsibilities and people's expectations on me, and I need to be transparent so that if I need help, I can get it early before it's too late.

But just because I managed to articulate all this and publish a book, it doesn't mean that somehow I have some supernatural ability to be perfect. As you can see, I am just as susceptible to the Myth of Motivation and the Gap like anybody else.

Transparency, however, should never be equated to weakness. I believe that it is in our strengths that we provide a beacon of hope for others. And it is in our weaknesses that we provide the opportunity for people to find strength for themselves.

The best part of using Re:LIFE for myself is that my own addictive mess does not have to define my personal value or self-image. Sure bad moments still creep up on me, but they are just momentary lapses into Gap-based thinking. Actually, my own mess gives me an opportunity to create and redeem Life in the communities around me.

I can't think of a better way to work through my own journey with Life than sharing it with others.

The difference before and after Nicaragua is, I now have a new frame of reference and a beacon to guide me when I get lost from time to time. When I find my Gap-based patterns getting the best of me, not only do I have those who love me enough to speak the sometimes painful truth and encouragement into my life, but I have a vision of a personal calling that brings back enough clarity to take the next few steps.

So what now for you? It's time to get to *your* relationship with Life.

My sincere hope is that you too will discover a vision and calling in Life that goes far beyond our expectations and versions of good. I hope that you can use Re:LIFE as a tool to find freedom from the Gaps and see Life for what it really is.

There is so much out there for us than just settling for good. May you embrace it all, change what you can, make it your own, and find the true Life we all are deep down searching for.

Your destiny is waiting!

NEXT STEPS: ADDITIONAL RESOURCES & ACKNOWLEDGMENTS

Free Personal Gap Evaluation

Over 70 Re:LIFE Strategies

Apprenticeship & Leadership Training

Podcasts & More!

Official Re:LIFE Web site and Ed Kang's blog:

www.giftofrelife.com

Contact Ed Kang and the Re:LIFE organization at:

relife@gmail.com

Re:LIFE contributes to "My Perfect Economy," an online article and blog Web site about creative capital for changing the world. My Perfect Economy is a division of the KCM Group of Companies and the KCM Venture Philanthropy Group.

www.myperfecteconomy.com

Proceeds from the sales of this book and any other Re:LIFE resources go to social enterprises and global humanitarian projects made possible by the Goliath Group of Companies. Special thanks to the Goliath Group for believing in me and making my first journey of compassion to Nicaragua possible.

www.goliathgroup.ca